Oxford International English

Emma Danihel

5

Workbook

OXFORD

1 Who am I?

All about me

Describing yourself

A

Write two adjectives next to the nouns below to describe yourself.

skin ______________________________

hair ______________________________

eyes ______________________________

nose ______________________________

voice ______________________________

personality ______________________________

clothes style ______________________________

B

Now use this information to write a paragraph about yourself.

Hi! My name is ______________ and I am ______________ years old.

I ______________________________

____

____

____

____

____

Making complex and compound sentences

Using 'but' correctly

A

Complete these sentences about yourself.

1 I like ______________________________, and I like ______________________________ in my free time.

2 I like eating ______________________, but I don't like eating ______________________________.

3 My favourite subject at school is ______________, but I don't enjoy ______________________________.

4 At the weekends, I don't like ______________________________, but I really enjoy ______________________________.

B

Choose between 'and' or 'but' to join each pair of clauses.

1 He reads a lot of books ____________ he has never been to a library.

2 She fell over ____________ hurt her leg.

3 This morning Maria missed the bus ____________ she was late for school.

4 Johan asked his friend to come to play ____________ he said he was too busy.

5 My sister is very friendly ____________ loves meeting people.

6 The boy shouted very loudly ____________ no one heard him.

C

Complete these sentences with a suitable ending.

1 I like ice-cream but ______________________________.

2 Tomas works very hard and ______________________________.

3 Tatiana loves her little sister but ______________________________.

4 Tatiana loves her little sister and ______________________________.

Suffixes

Words ending in '-er', '-or' and '-ar'

A

Use a dictionary to help you fill in the gaps with a suitable ending. Choose from '-or' / '-er'.

motivat ______	alligat ______	tut ______	batt ______
activat ______	mast ______	beekeep ______	admir ______
corrid ______	operat ______	adapt ______	tract ______
employ ______	build ______	sail ______	cultivat ______

B

Use a dictionary to match the verbs with their definitions. One has been done for you.

motivate	to control or manage something
cultivate	to adjust/change oneself to different conditions
activate	to provide (someone) with a reason for doing something
operate	to raise and grow
adapt	to regard with wonder, pleasure, approval
admire	to make something go

Choose three of the words above and put them into sentences.

1 ______________________________

2 ______________________________

3 ______________________________

C

Add '-er', '-or' or '-ar' to the examples below to make a noun. You might need to use your dictionary.

creat ______ err ______ teach ______ manag ______ cond ______

ang ______ calend ______ begg ______ sug ______ doct ______

Pronouns

Making pronouns clear

A

Read the poem 'Shoes by the door' on the next page. Underline nine pronouns in the poem. Write them out below and say which noun they have replaced. The first one has been done for you.

pronoun	noun
1 I	the poet
2	
3	
4	
5	
6	
7	
8	
9	

B

Change the underlined nouns or noun phrases into pronouns.

they I she me him he it we them us

1 I usually play football after school but today football was cancelled.
2 Our group won the trophy because our group won the most matches.
3 My friends were late so my friends missed the bus.
4 Johannes was thirsty so I gave Johannes some of my drink.
5 Maria didn't like her new shoes so she gave her new shoes to me.

C

Make your own sentences using the remaining five pronouns in the list.

1 ______________________________
2 ______________________________
3 ______________________________
4 ______________________________
5 ______________________________

Word pictures

Shoes by the door

Read the poem then answer the questions.

I left my shoes by the front door overnight
And in the morning they were full of draught

It slid in under the door, but the shoes were waiting
They drank it down and now it sat in their bellies

When I poked my toes and soles inside
My feet felt a silent unseen gulp.

by Michael Rosen

A

Connect the word to its correct definition.

stomachs or tummies

a current of air

to glide along without much effort

to prod, nudge or push something quite hard

to swallow/drink large amounts of something quickly.

the bottom of a foot

slide **poke** **sole** **draught** **gulp** **bellies**

B

Use words and phrases from the poem to support your answers to these questions.

1 Where did the poet leave his shoes? ____________________

2 Describe in your own words what you think the shoes felt like when the poet put them on in the morning. ____________________

____

3 How do you know? Now select words from the poem to support your answer.

____

Self-assessment on my learning

Unit 1 Who am I?

Name ______________________________

Date ______________________________

🙂 I understand and can do this well.

😐 I understand but I am not confident.

🙁 I don't understand and find this difficult.

Learning objective	🙂	😐	🙁
Reading poetry skills			
I can identify the point of view from which a story or poem is told.			
Writing skills			
I can use adjectives well in writing about myself.			
Language skills			
I understand and can use pronouns well.			
I can combine simple sentences to make compound and complex sentences using the conjunctions 'and' and 'but'.			
I understand the rules for using '-er', '-or' and '-ar' noun endings.			

I would like more help with ______________________________

____

____

____

Food, feasts and festivals

Paragraphs in non-fiction text

Winter festival

Read this passage about a festival in Canada.

The Carnival d'Hiver is the largest and most exciting winter festival in the world. It is held every year in Quebec City in Canada and runs from the end of January until the middle of February. It attracts almost 100,000 revellers from all around the world. There are so many thrilling activities for people of all ages, including snow-rafting, dogsled races, skating, sleighing and ice-sculpture contests. Children can even enjoy sliding down from the top of the ice palace! The last night of the Carnival is the most spectacular, as marching bands, clowns, dancers and street performers parade through the streets of Quebec in brightly coloured costumes, entertaining the delighted crowds lining the pavements.

A

Give the passage a suitable title and organize the text into three paragraphs. Make a line like this / in the text above where each new paragraph should begin.

Give each of the paragraphs a subheading.

Passage title: Winter Fun

Paragraph title 1: d'hiver

Paragraph title 2: Sliding down

Paragraph title 3: Carnival

B

Write three short paragraphs about a festival or carnival in your country. Include information about the time of year, how long it lasts, who goes and what you can do at it.

1 ______________________________

____

____

2 ______________________________

____

____

3 ______________________________

____

____

Onomatopoeia

C

Complete the following sentences with a suitable onomatopoeic word from the list provided.

bang	**whoosh**	**boom**	**whizz**	**sizzle**
bawl	**bark**	**flutter**	**crackling**	

There was a huge ____________ and then a ____________ as a firework flew up into the air. Then another mighty ____________ and a lot more ____________ as the sky exploded into a magnificent display of coloured lights. The baby next to me was shocked and started to ____________ while a frightened dog began to ____________ loudly. Later on, after the fireworks had finished, we stood by a ____________ fire, watching the sausages ____________ in a pan and watching snowflakes ____________ down from the sky.

A traditional story

Hansel and Gretel

Read this extract adapted from the story of Hansel and Gretel.

Hansel and Gretel were awoken from where they slept, underneath the tree, by the sweet sound of birdcall. Suddenly, a beautiful bird, with feathers as white as snow, swooped down from the sky and landed on a branch just above their heads. It put its head on one side and looked at them for a minute, then flew to a branch further away. The children thought the bird was the loveliest thing that they had ever seen, so they followed it. Each time they almost reached the bird it flew to another branch. On and on the children went, deeper and deeper into the forest, following the little bird.

Then, after a while, they came to a clearing, where there were no trees but a little house instead. The little bird flew over and sat upon the chimney pot.

This was no ordinary house, no ordinary house at all! This house had walls made of divine, golden, velvety gingerbread topped with the sweetest, most delicious, creamy, white icing. This house had windows of scrumptious, clear, melted sugar with gorgeous, delectable red and white striped candy canes as window frames.

A

Answer the comprehension questions using words and phrases from the text.

1 What woke the children up?

The birds woke up the childrens up.

2 What did the bird do when it landed on the branch above their heads?

It put its head on one side and looked at them for a minute, then flew to a branch further away.

3 Were the children surprised when they saw the house? How do you know?

The children was shocked and suprized.

4 What was around the clear sugar window panes of the house?

Red and white striped candy canes as window frames.

Finding words in the passage

B

In the passage a lot of synonyms for the word 'nice' are used. Find them in the passage then list them below in the correct place.

scr ______________________

b ______________________

sw ______________________

gor ______________________

dele ______________________

div ______________________

lo ______________________

deli ______________________

Suffixes and adverbs

Suffixes

A

Choose a word from the list below, adding the '-ful' or '-al' suffix to turn it into an adjective. Some sentences have more than one possibility.

inspiration delight colour power sensation

1 There was a ____________________ story about the Prime Minister in the newspaper today.

2 The professor gave an ____________________ lecture to her students.

3 When he sings he has a ____________________ voice.

4 The President was a ____________________ man.

5 The butterfly's wings were very ____________________.

Using adverbs

B

Change these adjectives into adverbs by adding '-ly' or '-ily'.

angry __________ cheerful __________

funny __________ anxious __________

C

Use the adverbs below to complete the sentences.

tunefully soundly neatly
smartly greedily heavily

1 The baby sleeps ____________________

2 My dad dresses ____________________

3 He writes ____________________

4 The rain is falling ____________________

5 He whistles ____________________

6 He ate ____________________

Self-assessment on my learning

Unit 2 Feasts and festivals

Name ______________________________

Date ______________________________

☺ I understand and can do this well.

😐 I understand but I am not confident.

☹ I don't understand and find this difficult.

Learning objective	☺	😐	☹
Reading skills			
I can use words and phrases from a story to answer comprehension questions			
I can read and evaluate a non-fiction text for organization.			
Writing skills			
I can use special vocabulary to write on a topic.			
Language skills			
I understand and can use suffixes and adverbs.			
I understand and can use onomatopoeia.			

I would like more help with ______________________________

3 Our blue planet

Adjectives, similes and metaphors

Matching words

A

Below are some nouns, verbs and adjectives often used to describe fire, wind, leaves or old people. Put each of the words in the box of the noun you think the word best describes. Some words could be able to go into more than one category.

autumn	cyclone	roaring	advanced	green	yellow
red	piercing	inferno	flickering	gnarled	ancient
draught	whistling	burning	pensioner	time-worn	blazing
falling	smoky	crunching	puff	rattling	icy
wrinkly	blowing	brittle	wise	crackling	breezy
chilly	tempest	golden-brown	retirement		

FIRE

OLD PEOPLE

WIND

LEAVES

B

Using the words on the opposite page to help you, write four short paragraphs describing wind, fire, old people and leaves.

1 ______________________________

____

____

2 ______________________________

____

____

3 ______________________________

____

____

4 ______________________________

____

____

C

Below are some words that could be used to describe the sea. Use a dictionary to match them with their definitions.

surf	a sudden forward movement by a natural force like the tide
spray	shine with soft, slightly wavering light
roaring	the line of foam formed by waves
surging	making a loud, deep, long sound
shimmer	liquid that is blown through the air to form tiny droplets

Using metaphor and simile to enrich fiction

The storm

Read the following passage.

Sat in my comfortable, old armchair, sipping hot, sugary tea, and warming my toes by my roaring fire, I could hear the sounds of the ferocious storm, raging all around me like a ravenous lion. My little home, stuck far out on the promontory, shook like a brittle leaf on a gnarled, old tree. The piercing wind whistled down the ancient chimney, rattling the plates on the dresser and bringing an icy chill with it. My time-worn fingers trembled as I bought the sweet, warming brew to my lips and remembered the storm, exactly like this one, thirty years before that had brought the stranger to my door. There had been an unexpected knock. "Who could be out in this tempest, Maggie?" I asked myself. I quickly opened the door and there he was. If only I had known then, what I know now.

A

Write out two examples of similes from the text.

B

Write out two examples of metaphors from the text.

C

How does the writer use similes and metaphors to paint a picture of the extreme weather conditions?

Metaphors and similes

A

Choose the best adjective to complete the following similes.

light **slippery** **old** **hard** **free** **white**

as ________ as snow as ________ as a rock

as ________ as a feather as ________ as the hills

as ________ as an eel as ________ as the wind

B

Choose the most suitable noun to complete these similes

an angel **a bomb** **cats and dogs** **a log**

1 The room looked like ________________ had hit it.

2 She sang like ________________.

3 The two brothers fight like ________________.

4 Last night, I slept like ________________.

C

Now choose the best nouns to complete the metaphors below.

a dream **a lion** **a rollercoaster** **a blanket**

1 She has the heart of ________________.

2 Life is ________________ which everyone has to get through.

3 I'm so happy, my life is a ________________.

4 ________________ of snow covered our village.

Commas and connectives

Where does the comma go?

A

In the following sentences, add the commas that have been missed out. Sometimes more than one is missing.

1 As it is your birthday I have decided to take you out.
2 If I had a dog I would call it Laddie.
3 Yesterday it was pouring with rain but today it is nice and sunny.
4 I went to see the new blockbuster at our local cinema but I didn't enjoy it.
5 As it is sunny today we are going to the beach but not for very long as I have work to do.
6 Alisha's sister the girl who is singing on the left is getting married in two weeks.

Which connective?

B

Choose the best connectives from the two in brackets, to complete the following sentences.

Example: We ate lunch early **because** we were going out. (so/because)

1 He was tired ____________________ he went to bed early. (so/because)
2 I wasn't surprised ____________________ he wanted to be a doctor. (that/so)
3 I will need to buy more wood ____________________ winter will be here soon. (if/because)
4 We will stay at home ____________________ it rains tomorrow. (if/because)
5 He stood on the box ____________________ he wanted to see over the fence. (so/because)

Self-assessment on my learning

Unit 3 Our blue planet

Name ______________________________

Date ______________________________

☺ I understand and can do this well.

😐 I understand but I am not confident.

☹ I don't understand and find this difficult.

Learning objective	☺	😐	☹
Reading skills			
I can identify unfamiliar words, explore definitions and use new words.			
I can comment on a writer's use of language.			
Language skills			
I can discuss metaphorical expressions and figures of speech.			
I can begin to use commas to separate clauses within sentences.			
I can investigate clauses within sentences and how they are connected.			

I would like more help with ______________________________

4 Stories and comic strips

Turning a story into cartoons

Reading comprehension

Read this extract adapted from *The Cartoonist.*

"I don't know what you do up there," his mom said, watching him.

"I study."

"Well, it is not healthy – no windows, no air. Mr Wilkins has an old window in his garage. Maybe I could get him to..."

"I like it just the way it is," Alfie said quickly.

"Well, you ought to be more like Bubba," she said, eyeing him critically. "When he was your age he was outside every day, passing a football, dribbling a basket ball..."

"Stealing a baseball," Alma added.

His mother ignored Alma. "You're never going to be on a team," she urged.

"That's true," he said.

"But, Alfie, everybody wants to be on a team!"

From *The Cartoonist* by Betsy Byars

A

Give evidence from the text for your answers to A and B.

1 Why does Alfie's mother not like him spending so much time in the loft?

2 Did Alfie's sister, Alma, have the same opinion about Bubba as Alfie's mother? How do you know?

B

What do you think?

1 Why doesn't Alfie want Mr Wilkins to come to put a window in the attic?

2 Alfie's mother says that everybody wants to be on a team. Do you think that Alfie wants to be on a team? How do you know?

Writing new scenes

C

Use these boxes to change the text into cartoon form by drawing Alfie, his mother and sister with what they are saying in speech bubbles.

Adverbs

Descriptive adverbs

A

Find two '-ly' adverbs the writer used in the extract from *The Cartoonist*.

B

The adverbs below have similar meaning to the ones used in *The Cartoonist*. Choose a good adverb from the list to fill in each gap in the dialogue.

sullenly impatiently severely rudely
sadly strongly suspiciously

1 "I don't know what you do up there," his mother said ___________________

2 "I study," he replied ___________________

3 "Well, you ought to be more like Bubba," she said ___________________

4 "You're never going to be on a team," she said ___________________

5 "That's true," he replied ___________________

Prepositions

A

Fill in the gaps with a suitable preposition from the list below. You can use each preposition only once so cross them out as you use them.

up above for about on along at through inside against in down on across out after into to from off

Leila was walking __________ her road, __________ her way home, thinking __________ the lovely dinner waiting __________ home __________ her, when suddenly she heard a meowing __________ her head. She looked __________ and saw her neighbour's kitten stuck __________ the tree. She tried to call it __________ but it was too afraid. Leila then went __________ the road and knocked __________ her neighbour's door. __________ Leila explained the problem __________ her neighbour, the neighbour came __________ of his house and went __________ his garden __________ a side gate. He took a ladder from __________ his shed and put the ladder __________ the tree. Moments later the neighbour took the little kitten carefully __________ the tree, and carrying it gently, came __________ the ladder.

B

Write suitable sentences which you can end with the following prepositional phrases.

1 onto the wall

____

2 through the round window

____

3 into the swimming pool

____

4 up the stairs

____

5 out of the school gates

____

Using adverbs

Adverbial phrases

A

Add one of the adverbs in the list to the adverbs in each of the sentences to make an adverbial phrase.

quite **rather** **very** **surprisingly** **extremely**

1 My sister spoke to me __________ rudely.
2 "Get out of here," Massoud said __________ menacingly.
3 Carlos felt __________ poorly, so he didn't go to school.
4 Although he did no revision, Anush did __________ brilliantly in his exams.
5 It wasn't her best result, but she was still __________ happy with the result.

B

Turn the words below into adverbs.

pain __________	aggression __________
obedience __________	misery __________
joy __________	excitement __________
gracefulness __________	mistake __________
merriment __________	humour __________

C

Make three sentences using adverbs from Exercise B.

1 ______________________________

____

2 ______________________________

____

3 ______________________________

____

Self-assessment on my learning

Unit 4 Stories and comic strips

Name ______________________________

Date ______________________________

☺ I understand and can do this well.

😐 I understand but I am not confident.

☹ I don't understand and find this difficult.

Learning objective	☺	😐	☹
Reading skills			
I can identify unfamiliar words and explore definitions.			
I can explore features of different fiction genres.			
Writing skills			
I can write new scenes into a story.			
Language skills			
I can understand and use adverbs.			
I can identify and use prepositions.			

I would like more help with ______________________________

____

____

____

5 World change makers

Prepositions

Choosing the correct prepositions

A

Complete the following paragraph by adding a preposition from the list below. Once you have used one, cross it out.

with towards in from of at by of from by for in

Professor Muhammad Yanus started the Grameen Bank ____________ Bangladesh ____________ 1983 because he wanted to help poor people escape ____________ poverty ____________ providing them ____________ loans which were suitable ____________ them. ____________ these humble beginnings, the Grameen Bank has advanced ____________ the front ____________ a growing world movement aiming ____________ ending world poverty ____________ lending small amounts ____________ money at low interest.

B

Make sentences of your own using the following prepositions.

against between beyond

1 ____

____

2 ____

____

3 ____

____

Complex sentences

Using a comma to separate clauses

A

Rewrite the sentences below to include the information in the brackets. Remember to include all the correct punctuation.

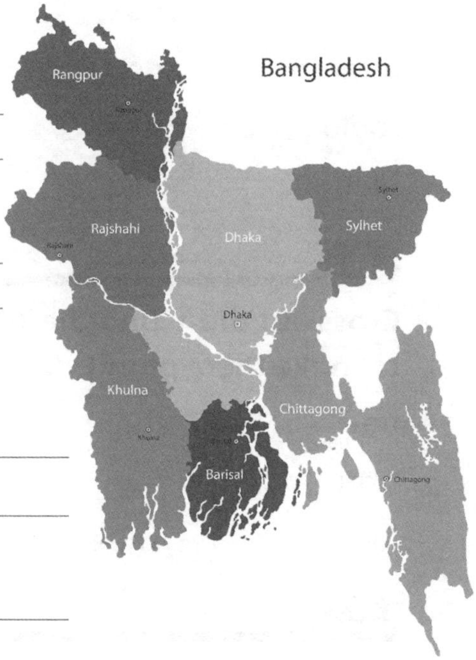

1 Muhammad Yunus opened The Grameen Bank in 1983. (which means Village Bank) ______________________________

____

2 He wanted to help basket weavers to find a suitable loan for themselves. (who were very poor) ______________________________

____

3 There is a world movement that is aiming to put an end to world poverty. (which The Grameen Bank is part of)

____

____

4 Muhammed Yunus won the Nobel Prize in 2006. (which is one of the most prestigious awards) ______________________________

____

B

Add the missing commas to the following sentences.

1 Yesterday I went for a nice long walk along the canal.

2 My best friend who is a year older than me is going to a different school next year.

3 In the end we decided to go home early.

4 By this time tomorrow I will be on a train to Paris which is where my cousin lives.

C

Finish these sentences in your own words. Don't forget to add the correct punctuation.

1 Since last year ______________________________

2 ______________________________ instead of my best friend.

3 ______________________________ next to the sea.

Making plurals

Following spelling patterns

A

Add '-s' or '-es' to the following nouns to make them plural.

lunch ____	box ____	cat ____	dish ____	door ____
tomato ____	day ____	watch ____	table ____	wish ____
radio ____	tree ____	glass ____	pear ____	book ____
piano ____	pea ____			

B

Cross out the 'f' and the 'y' and add '-ies', '-s' or '-ves' to these nouns to make them plural.

half ____	fly ____	party ____	story ____	berry ____
tray ____	toy ____	baby ____	calf ____	jelly ____
lady ____	knife ____	curry ____	day ____	

C

Some plural nouns do not follow clear rules. What are the plurals of the following nouns?

child	____________	foot	____________
tooth	____________	oasis	____________
sheep	____________	man	____________
woman	____________	fish	____________
mouse	____________	person	____________

Prefixes

The useful prefix

A

Complete the following sentences by choosing a word below then adding a prefix to make it negative.

comfort **satisfied** **popular** **polite** **likely**

Example: happy He was very unhappy about the situation.

1 He was quite ______________ with the other children at school.

2 The food critic felt ______________ with his meal at the five star restaurant.

3 It is the middle of summer so it is ______________ to rain tomorrow.

4 The shop assistant was rather ______________ to the lady making a complaint.

5 After eating such a big meal so late at night, I felt a lot of ______________ when I went to bed.

B

Find out what the following prefixes mean and write an explanation.

Example: 'pre-' = before

geo ______________ mis ______________ tele ______________

bi ______________ re ______________

C

Use your dictionary to list two more words that use these prefixes:

pre-	geo-	mis-	tele-	bi-
prehistoric	geography	misfortune	telephone	binoculars

Planning your writing project

Writing a biography

A

Remembering your writing workshop from Unit 5, name three features of biographies.

1 ______________________

2 ______________________

3 ______________________

B

Plan your own biography of someone that you admire. It could be a sports person, a film star, a politician or a member of your family. Before you write your biography, you should collect information.

Where/when were they born? ______________________

Where did they go to school or university? ______________________

Where have they lived and worked? ______________________

____

What is their character and reputation? ______________________

____

Is there something special that they have achieved? ______________________

____

Why do you admire them? ______________________

____

C

Now write down the titles of the paragraphs of your short biography. You can use more or less than four.

Paragraph 1 ______________________

Paragraph 2 ______________________

Paragraph 3 ______________________

Paragraph 4 ______________________

Self-assessment on my learning

Unit 5 World change makers

Name ____________________

Date ____________________

☺ I understand and can do this well.

😐 I understand but I am not confident.

☹ I don't understand and find this difficult.

Learning objective	☺	😐	☹
Writing skills			
I can map out writing to plan the structure of a biography.			
Language skills			
I can identify prepositions and know how to use them.			
I can use the comma to separate clauses in compound sentences and to clarify meaning in complex sentences.			
I understand spelling patterns for pluralization.			
I can use prefixes to create negative words and to make up new words.			

I would like more help with ____________________

____

____

____

6 Sport and health

Using punctuation and vocabulary

Using commas

A

Read this information text from a children's encyclopaedia. You will notice that there are no commas. Insert the commas that have been missed out in the text.

Tennis is a game played by either two players known as singles or four players called doubles. If a man and a woman play against another man and woman then it is called mixed doubles. Each player has a racket. There is a hollow rubber ball which is covered with felt. The players aim to hit the ball over a net into their opponent's court in such a way that it is too difficult for the opponent to return the ball back.

Tennis originated from England in the late nineteenth century. Then it was known as Lawn Tennis. Today tennis is played by millions of people all over the world. There are many different competitions but the four most important are known as Grand Slams. These are the Australian Open French Open Wimbledon and the US Open.

Special vocabulary

B

Notice that the underlined words are specialized vocabulary relating specifically to the topic being described. Think of another sport and make a list of specialized vocabulary: words which relate to that sport. Use a dictionary or encyclopaedia to help you.

Sport ____________

____________ ____________ ____________ ____________

____________ ____________ ____________ ____________

C

Using your list of specialized vocabulary write your own information text about the sport you have chosen. You might want to include the following information:

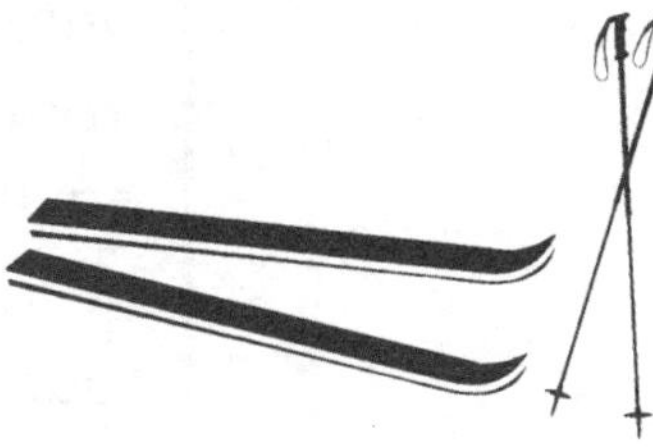

1 How to play the game

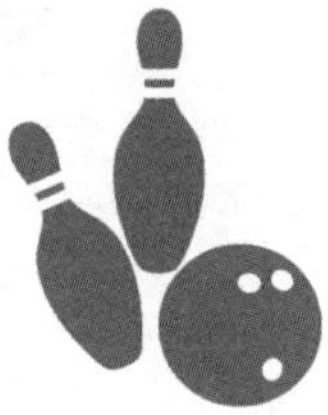

2 Where the game originally came from

3 Where it is most popular now

4 Important tournaments or competitions

5 The best players of the game

Interviews

Tennis interview

A

Read this interview with the tennis player Danek Hlavacek and answer the questions below.

JB You were obviously one of the favourites to win, so why have you pulled out of Wimbledon this year?

DH Unfortunately, it's all down to my back injury. I was suffering from really bad back pain in the French Open and I just haven't fully recovered enough yet. I'm really devastated because I love the atmosphere at Wimbledon – it's the tournament I enjoy playing at the most.

JB So who is your favourite to win Wimbledon this year?

DH Well, it is really difficult to say. Nadal and Federer are both great players, of course, but neither has been on good form for the last few months. Ferrer has had a really good year, but he's all about speed and he prefers clay courts to the soft grass courts of Wimbledon. So perhaps this will finally be Murray's year. He's certainly been playing really well recently and he's so eager to succeed at Wimbledon.

1 Why did Hlavacek pull out of Wimbledon? ____________________

____

2 Why was Hlavecek unhappy about having to pull out of the Wimbledon?

____

____

3 Who did Hlavacek think would win Wimbledon? ____________________

B

What do you think?

1 According to Hlavacek, what is the difference between playing on clay courts and playing on grass courts? ____________________

____

____

2 Why does Hlavacek suggest that Murray is so keen to win Wimbledon?

____

____

____

Direct or reported speech

C

Decide which of the sentences below are direct speech and which are reported speech. Ring the correct answer.

1 "Why have you pulled out of Wimbledon?" she asked. Direct/Indirect
2 "It's sadly all down to my back," he replied. Direct/Indirect
3 He said that it was a problem he had been suffering from at the French Open. Direct/Indirect
4 He told JB that it was a shame because he enjoyed playing at Wimbledon the most. Direct/Indirect

D

Change JB'S second question in the text to reported speech.

____

____

____

Keeping a diary

Recording what happens

A

Sailor Laura Dekker kept a diary of her solo journey. List three features of diary writing.

1 ______________________________

2 ______________________________

3 ______________________________

B

Write a short diary over the next seven days recording some of the things that happen to you each day. Remember to use informal language.

DAY 1 ______________________________

DAY 2 ______________________________

DAY 3 ______________________________

DAY 4 ______________________________

DAY 5 ______________________________

DAY 6 ______________________________

DAY 7 ______________________________

Self-assessment on my learning

Unit 6 Sport and health

Name ______________________________

Date ______________________________

☺ I understand and can do this well.

😐 I understand but I am not confident.

☹ I don't understand and find this difficult.

Learning objective	☺	😐	☹
Reading skills			
I can find information in a passage.			
Writing skills			
I can write a diary.			
Language skills			
I understand direct and indirect speech.			
I can use special vocabulary.			
I can use commas correctly.			

I would like more help with ______________________________

____

____

____

7 Making the news

Creating opposites, making comparisons

Prefixes for opposites

A

The prefixes 'un-', 'dis-', 'in-', il-' and' ir-' all mean 'not' and are used to create the opposite meaning of a word. Choose the right prefix to connect to the words below to make the opposite meaning.

dis un in il ir

______ happy	______ trust	______ like	______ legal
______ beatable	______ even	______ deserved	______ content
______ relevant	______ equal	______ well	______ obey
______ obedient	______ logical	______ dress	______ popular
______ well	______ please	______ likely	______ pleasant

Forming the comparative and superlative

Look at these examples of comparatives and superlatives.

adjective	**comparative**	**superlative**
big	bigger	biggest
bright	brighter	brightest
white	whiter	whitest
angry	angrier	angriest
careful	more careful	most careful
confident	more confident	most confident

B

Using the examples opposite to help you, write the spelling rules for forming the following comparative and superlative forms.

1 A one-syllable adjective

Example: 'bright': add '-er' or '-est' to the end of the word.

2 A one-syllable adjective ending in 'e'

____

3 A one-syllable adjective ending with a single consonant with a single vowel before it

____

4 A two-syllable adjective

____

5 A two-syllable adjective ending with 'y'

____

6 Adjectives with three or more syllables

____

C

Write six more adjectives to give an example of each of the above rules.

1 ____________ **2** ____________ **3** ____________

4 ____________ **5** ____________ **6** ____________

D

The following adjectives are irregular and do not follow the rules. Complete the comparative and superlative forms in the spaces provided.

adjective	**comparative**	**superlative**
good		
bad		
far		
little		
many		

Sounds the same but different meaning

They're, their or there.

A

Fill in the gaps with 'they're', 'their', or 'there'.

1 As my neighbours were on holiday, I watered ________________ garden for them.

2 ________________ was a huge thunderstorm in the night.

3 I looked in his bedroom, but John wasn't ________________

4 We are going to Eshe and Haji's house tonight as ________________ cooking us a special dinner.

5 The children looked everywhere for ________________ ball but they couldn't find it anywhere.

6 A week ago my friend's family went on ________________ holidays to Greece and ________________ having a great time ________________!

Where, we're, wear or were

B

Fill in the gaps with 'where', 'we're', 'wear 'or 'were'.

1 ________________ did you say you ________________ going tomorrow night?

2 We ________________ going to the cinema but now ________________ going to the theatre instead.

3 What are you going to ________________ to the theatre?

4 I want to ________________ my long, black dress, but I don't know ________________ it is.

5 ________________ you happy when you found out your parents ________________ taking you on holiday?

Idioms

Everyday sayings

A

Rewrite these sentences using one of the idioms below.

1 They found a solution *right at the last minute.* ____________________

2 All the noise next door is *making me so cross.* ____________________

3 We go out to dinner together about *once a year.* ____________________

4 It was raining *really heavily* all the time while we were camping.
____

5 My father reversed into the garden wall and had to pay *a lot of money* to get the car fixed. ____________________

6 My English homework was *really easy.* ____________________

at the eleventh hour	**an arm and a leg**	**once in a blue moon**
driving me up the wall	**cats and dogs**	**a piece of cake**

B

Use one of the words below to complete the following idioms and then match each of the idioms with their correct definition.

hit thick hat teeth dumps weather

Idiom	Definition
1 by the skin of one's ____________	to leave
2 at the drop of a ____________	feel sick or unwell
3 under the ____________	narrowly or barely
4 down in the ____________	both good and bad times
5 to ____________ the road	instantly, without hesitation
6 through ____________ and thin	miserable, unhappy

Persuasive language in adverts

A perfect holiday

Advertisements are a type of persuasive writing. They appeal to your feelings by using strong descriptive words. Read this newspaper advert.

European Holiday

Nothing can possibly compare with the wonderful elegance of a fantastic holiday in Europe. Discover amazing and delightful destinations brimming with cultural and scenic splendour. Make 2015 the year that you cruise the sublime Scottish shores, relax on the tranquil, glorious shores of the Italian lakes or experience the breathtakingly, spectacular mountain range of the Swiss Alps. Whatever you decide, you're certain to find your perfect European getaway so do not hesitate, do not miss out on this once in a life time trip, book now to save disappointment later.

A

Circle all the strong words used in the advertisement, then find their synonyms in a thesaurus or dictionary.

Example: sublime - synonyms: glorious, splendorous, superb

B

Fill in the gaps in this advertisement with suitable strong and persuasive words.

Join us for an ________________ journey to ________________ (fill in the name of your country here) full of ________________ highlights. This will surely be a ________________ holiday. You will see ________________ scenery and some of the most ________________ cities of the world. Our hotels offer the most ________________ accommodation at ________________ prices. Truly, this will be a ________________ experience for you.

C

On a separate piece of paper, write your own advertisement using suitable language to persuade people to come on holiday to a place or area in your country.

Self-assessment on my learning

Unit 7 Making the news

Name ______________________________

Date ______________________________

☺ I understand and can do this well.

😐 I understand but I am not confident.

☹ I don't understand and find this difficult.

Learning objective	☺	😐	☹
Writing skills			
I can organize and write a newspaper advertisement using persuasive language.			
Language skills			
I can investigate ways of creating opposites and comparatives.			
I can identify different grammatical homophones.			
I can identify and use a number of idiomatic phrases.			

I would like more help with ______________________________

____

____

____

8 Flying high

Verbs

Get the verb right

A

Add 'was' or 'were' to complete the following sentences.

1 We ______________ on our way home when we met Katarina and Maria.

2 They ______________ going to the swimming pool.

3 The cinema ______________ showing our favourite film.

4 The children ______________ playing in the park.

5 Mum ______________ cross because we ______________ late home.

B

Complete the sentences by putting the verbs in brackets into the correct tenses.

1 She ______________ (drive) to the shops when her car ______________ (break down)

2 I ______________ (run) to school this morning because I ______________ (be) late.

3 Mariam's brother ______________ (be) three years older than her sister.

4 We ______________ (eat) our lunch before we went to the park.

5 Dom ______________ (feel) sick when I ______________ (call) him this morning so we are not ______________ (go) out.

C

Change these sentences from the present to the past, or the past to the present.

1 Anya gets up at 6 am every morning and eats her breakfast before walking to school.

____

____

2 I was running late so I was eating very quickly.

____

D

Complete this passage by putting the verbs in brackets into the correct form.

Tania suddenly ____________ (open) her eyes and ____________ (sit) up in her bed. There ____________ (be) the noise again. She definitely ____________ (hear) something this time. She ____________ (be) sure if the noise ____________ (come) from the other bedrooms. Nervously, she ____________ (drag) herself from her nice warm bed and ____________ (creep) noiselessly to her bedroom door.

She ____________ (decide) not to turn on the lights but instead slowly and silently she ____________ (open) the door. Then, she ____________ (see) her younger brother ____________ (shuffle) towards the kitchen to ____________ (get) a midnight snack!

Synonyms for powerful stories

A

Find a synonym from the list below to match the correct word in the box.

sultry	**chilly**	**devour**	**nibble**	**furious**	**radiant**
grin	**merry**	**dim**	**blubber**	**sneak**	**cranky**

cold ______	creep ______	cry ______
dull ______	bright ______	irritable ______
happy ______	smile ______	bite ______
angry ______	hot ______	gobble ______

B

Find a synonym for each of the underlined words in the following sentences.

1 The sudden noise startled the children. ______

2 "I don't want to go for a walk," my sister moaned. ______

3 The plane rolled down the runway. ______

4 May was very agitated when she heard the news. ______

5 He grabbed my hand to save me from slipping. ______

C

In the story extract about Tania on the previous page, find synonyms that mean 'to walk quietly'.

______

______

D

Find one synonym for each of the words below then write one sentence using each synonym.

1 bright ____________________

____

____

2 huge ____________________

____

____

3 strangely ____________________

____

____

E

Replace the underlined words in the passage with synonyms which are stronger and more descriptive.

"What's that?" said Sara. ______________

"What's what?" said Anika. ______________

"That!" said Sara. ______________

"Oh, I don't know. It's nothing," said Anika. "Go back to sleep." ______________

"I definitely saw something move outside the tent," said Sara. ______________

"What's that unpleasant sound?" said Sara.

____

"I don't know," said Anika beginning to feel unhappy. ______________

"It's coming closer," said Sara. ______________

"I know," said Anika feeling very unhappy.

____

The girls were both scared. ______________

"Surprise," said Mario, Sara's little brother, poking his head through the tent mischievously.

Spelling word endings

Word endings

A

Remember the rules for spelling words ending '-ed' and '-ing'. Complete the table below.

comply	complied	complying
flip	flipped	flipping
wade	waded	wading
fake	________	________
________	gripped	________
________	________	trimming
________	tamed	________
supply	________	________
mop	________	________
snore	________	________

B

Fill in the gaps of the following sentences with a suitable verb ending in '-ed' or '-ing'.

We ____________ slowly in our hot air balloon over the top of the forest, closer and closer towards the clearing. It was ____________ dark and cold and my heart was ____________ so fast I was ____________ that I would faint. We were dangerously close to ____________ into the trees below us. "There it is," ____________ Alberto. We ____________ at each other and ____________.

"Quick, get the ropes ready," Alberto ____________.

"OK!" I ____________. But just as we got close to the landing spot the balloon jolted and we ____________.

Self-assessment on my learning

Unit 8 Flying high

Name ______________________________

Date ______________________________

☺ I understand and can do this well.

😐 I understand but I am not confident.

☹ I don't understand and find this difficult.

Learning objective	☺	😐	☹
Language skills			
I understand and can change the tense of sentences.			
I understand and can use a range of synonyms.			
I can spell words using '-ed' and 'ing'.			

I would like more help with ______________________________

____

____

____

9 Tales and legends

Pronouns

A

The pronouns in the following sentences have been written incorrectly. Write the correct pronoun at the end of the sentence.

1 She gave all her's friends a sweet each. __________

2 My neighbours grow a lot of apple trees in they're garden. __________

3 That pencil is my. __________

4 I don't like going to my cousins' house because there cats are very mean. __________

5 Their house is bigger than our's. __________

6 Tchang's mother had three pearls of his own. __________

B

Complete these sentences by adding a suitable pronoun in the gaps.

1 The children gave __________ books to the teacher at the end of __________ lesson.

2 The group of climbers set __________ the difficult task of climbing the hill at night time.

3 You can give the biscuits to your friends if __________ want __________.

4 My sister and I have short hair but __________ is shorter than __________.

Tchang and the Pearl Dragon

The tale of the missing commas

A

Add the missing commas to this text taken from the Tchang story.

Suddenly a great green dragon rose from the water. Even to Tchang who had never met a dragon before its tiny wings seemed too small for its body. Set in its forehead was a gorgeous pearl…

On a throne at the end of the hall sat the Great Wizard. He glared down at Tchang. "Well?" he bellowed. "What do you want boy? I will only answer THREE questions. If you ask me four I won't answer any of them."

There was his poor mother's question then the old woman's question then the old man's question and then the Pearl Dragon's question. For his own sake as well as his mother's he desperately wanted to know the answer to the first question – but he also knew he couldn't let his friends down. So he answered sadly, "Then I will only ask you three."

Tchang and the Pearl Dragon
by Andy Blackford

B

Write out the rule for three of the different uses of commas within the story of Tchang above.

Rule 1 ______________________________

Rule 2 ______________________________

Rule 3 ______________________________

Apostrophes

Possession or shortened form

A

In the following sentences put a circle around apostrophes of possession and underline apostrophes showing a shortened form.

1 They're going to Gomez's to ask him if he wants to play football.
2 The girls' school up the road isn't very big.
3 I wasn't looking where I was going and knocked into the man's shoulder.
4 The garage said they would be able to fix my aunty's car by Wednesday.
5 My brother's room is always untidy.

B

Add the missing apostrophes to the following sentences.

1 My childrens school isnt far from our house.
2 All the animals cages in the zoo need to be cleaned while theyre eating.
3 Ill have my dinner then get down to my homework.
4 Its raining so Im going to take the dog for a walk later.
5 At Khans party all the kids enjoyed his mums chocolate cake so much, they had second helpings!

C

Put the following words into appropriate sentences.

1 bear's ______________________________

____

2 bees' ______________________________

____

3 girl's ______________________________

____

Writing genres

Which genre?

A

Look at these opening sentences and choose the genre you think that they belong to.

autobiography news information diary

legend instructions suspense biography fable

1 Once upon a time, there was a hare who was always showing off about how fast he could run.

____

2 Long, long ago, in China, there was a boy called Houyi.

____

3 Dear diary,
We got up late and had mum's special eggy bread – I love Saturday mornings!

____

4 John Taylor was born on 27 May 1947, in a small village called Sawston.

____

5 First take four eggs and crack them into a large mixing dish.

____

6 As I edged nervously closer and closer to the door, the pitiful, moaning sound behind it, became stronger and chilled my heart to ice.

____

7 My earliest recollection was the day of my fourth birthday.

____

8 The President to announce new measures to combat litter on streets

____

9 The Cheetah is a member of the feline or cat family and is found in Asia, Africa and Indonesia.

____

Writing a traditional tale

Getting the opening right

When you are writing a traditional tale or legend, you want to set the scene at the beginning and you want to make your opening sentence exciting so that the reader wants to read on.

Read this opening sentence.

Long, long ago there was a lazy hare who was always boasting, to anyone that would listen, that he was the fastest of all creatures.

A

Write two more opening sentences for a traditional tale or legend. You can invent your own story or tell a tale that you know.

1 ______________________________

____

2 ______________________________

____

Making a plan to write a traditional tale or legend.

You can follow your opening sentence with the following structure:

Problem/action	A tortoise challenges the hare to a race.
Resolution	The hare is so far in front he decides to have a rest and falls asleep. So the tortoise, who is running at a slow, even pace, wins the race.
Ending/moral	Slow and steady is best and don't show off.

B

Write your own plan for a traditional tale or legend.

____

____

____

____

____

Self-assessment on my learning

Unit 9 Tales and legends

Name ______________________________

Date ______________________________

☺ I understand and can do this well.

😐 I understand but I am not confident.

☹ I don't understand and find this difficult.

Learning objective	☺	😐	☹
Reading skills			
I can explore the text features of traditional tales and legends.			
Writing skills			
I can write my own legend or fable using typical features of the genre.			
Language skills			
I can use pronouns, making clear to what or whom they refer.			
I can use commas to separate clauses within sentences and clarify meaning in complex sentences.			
I can use apostrophes for both possession and shortened forms.			

I would like more help with ______________________________

____

____

____

10 Fabulous future

Fantastic facts about the future

Reading for understanding

A

Read this passage and answer the questions on page 57.

File Edit View History Bookmarks Help

With the recent advancements in technology, human-like robots look set to play an increasingly important role in the lives of humans. They might, in the near future, take the place of company receptionists; care workers to the elderly; home helps; or even become carers to our children.

Research has shown that, far from being distressed by contact with humanoid robots, the young generation sympathize with them and that they personified them with certain of their own attributes.

Young children, between the ages of four and five, were put in a room with a humanoid robot which was secretly being controlled by scientists in another room using remote control. When questioned later, the children believed that the robot had portrayed feelings, that it had shown empathy towards them and that it was capable of being their friend. The children also felt it deserved fair treatment.

1 What are some of the jobs the article suggests robots might be doing in the future?

______ ______ ______ ______

2 What kind of relationship did the young children believe they had with the robot?

______

______

3 Did the children perceive the robot as an inanimate (lifeless) object? How do you know?

______

______

B

What do you think?

1 Why did the scientists operate the robot by remote control in another room?

______

______

2 Why would this experiment not work so well with older children or adults?

______

______

3 Would it have made a difference to the experiments if the robot had not been in a recognisable, human form?

______

______

C

Replace the underlined words in the text with one of the words below. You need to keep the same meaning as the original word.

appreciate ______
troubled ______
shown ______
warmth ______
humanized ______
part ______
just ______
properties ______

Choosing the right pronoun

Pronouns

A

In the following sentences replace the underlined words with one personal pronoun.

1 The new girl started school today. ___________

2 My neighbour's children were playing in my neighbour's children's garden. ___________ ___________

3 My family are going on my family's holiday in July. ___________ ___________

4 I gave the children back the children's ball.

___________ ___________

5 My cat put my cat's head on my lap and purred. ___________

B

Underline the correct possessive pronoun to complete the sentences.

1 These are my shoes; (yours/mine) are under the table.
2 I finished my classwork in time but Jasmine didn't finish (her/hers).
3 Your teacher is much less strict than (our's/ours).
4 I loved my meal but Ali didn't like (his/yours).
5 Maria said that it was (her/hers) book not Sonia's.

C

Unscramble the possessive pronouns below and write a sentence for each.

srehti ____

____

sryuo ____

____

ish ____

____

Formal and informal writing

Writing a letter of complaint

A

Some of the informal language used in this letter of complaint is not correct for the task. Underline what you think should be changed.

Hi Mr Smith,

I totally loved the classical performance of *The Planets* that your theatre's orchestra performed the day before yesterday, it was cool but one thing made me so mad. There I was, listening intensely when all these guys came in late, making a noise and annoying everyone with their chatting.

Mr Smith, please, I mean, that totally ruined the whole thing for me. Surely, once the music has begun it is ok to expect total silence from the audience.

In future, I implore you to make it your policy that once the orchestra is ready to begin, that you close the doors and allow no one in or out until the interval. Keep the doors shut! And don't let some people disturb other people.

Thanks a lot,
Max Oyed

B

Write out the language features for writing formal letters.

Feature 1 ______________________________

____

Feature 2 ______________________________

____

Feature 3 ______________________________

____

Feature 4 ______________________________

____

C

Rewrite the letter, removing all the inappropriate language and replacing it with more suitable, formal language.

Self-assessment on my learning

Unit 10 Fabulous future

Name ______________________________

Date ______________________________

☺ I understand and can do this well.

😐 I understand but I am not confident.

☹ I don't understand and find this difficult.

Learning objective	☺	😐	☹
Reading skills			
I can read and evaluate a non-fiction text for organization.			
Writing skills			
I can understand and use special vocabulary to write for a specific purpose.			
Language skills			
I understand and can use pronouns.			
I can choose appropriate words.			

I would like more help with ______________________________

____

____

____

Word cloud dictionary

Aa

ace *adjective* very good

acetate *noun* a transparent sheet of plastic that you can draw on

achievement *noun* something that you succeed in doing

activist *noun* a person who is active in a programme for political change

advance *noun* improvement or progress

adventurer *noun* a person who goes on unusual, exciting or dangerous journeys

alien *adjective* foreign

altimeter *noun* an instrument used in aircraft for showing the height above sea level

angle *noun* a point of view

angry *adjective* feeling anger (a strong feeling that you want to quarrel or fight with someone)

animate *verb* give life to

animated *adjective* (for a film) made by photographing a series of still pictures and showing them rapidly one after another, so they appear to move

animator *noun* a person who animates films

anthology *noun* a collection of poems, stories, or songs in one book

apartheid *noun* a political system in which only some people have full political rights, such as white people in South Africa

armour *noun* a metal suit to protect you from danger

artwork *noun* photographs and illustrations in books, newspapers and magazines

astronaut *noun* someone who travels in a spacecraft

avocado *noun* a tropical fruit with a soft pale green oily flesh, often eaten in salads

Aztec people *noun* members of the civilization that was dominant in Mexico before the Spanish Conquest of the sixteenth century

Bb

ban *verb* forbid people to do something

bare *adjective* not covered with anything

base *noun* in baseball, one of the four positions that a player must reach in order to score points

baseball *noun* a game invented in the USA

bellow *verb* roar or shout loudly and deeply

blacken *verb* to make something black

blast off *verb* when a rocket is launched, it blasts off (takes off)
bleary *adjective* bleary eyes are tired and do not see clearly
Blue Planet *noun* planet Earth is called 'blue' because it looks blue from space
bluntly *adverb* directly, not trying to be polite
bold *adjective* brave and adventurous
booster *noun* an additional engine or rocket for a spacecraft
brainstorm *verb* suggest ideas and then discuss them
brave *adjective* ready to face danger or suffering
break a story *idiom* write and publish a new important news report
brittle *adjective* easy to break
bronze *noun* a yellow brown colour, like the metal mixture of copper and tin
bulge *verb* stick out or swell
burner *noun* the part of a hot air balloon that produces a flame
burrow *verb* make a hole or tunnel by digging
busses *noun, plural* large road vehicles that carry passengers
by the way *idiom* an expression used as an aside, an extra

Cc

cable *noun* a thick metal wire
cacao *noun* a tropical tree with a seed from which cocoa and chocolate are made
calendar *noun* a year planner
camera *noun* a piece of equipment for taking photographs, films, or television pictures
cannonball *noun* a heavy metal or stone ball fired from a cannon
canopy *noun* the fabric part of the balloon that fills with hot air
captor *noun* somebody who takes a person or an animal as a prisoner
career *noun* what a person does to make progress in their life, work or sport
career *verb* move with great speed around a corner or bend
cargo *noun* goods carried in a ship or aircraft
carnivore *noun* an animal that eats meat
cartoon *noun* a series of drawings that tell a story
cascade *verb* fall down like the water in a waterfall
cause *noun* reason, a thing that makes something happen
CE *noun* Common Era
ceramics *noun* the art of making pottery
ceremonial *adjective* to do with a ceremony, or used in a ceremony
championship *noun* a contest or competition in a game or sport

change *noun* the money that you get back if you pay more than the amount that something costs
chilli *noun* the hot-tasting pod of a pepper plant
circumnavigate *verb* sail completely round something, such as the world
civilization *noun* a society or culture with an organized way of life
clay *noun* a sticky kind of earth, used for making bricks and pottery
clever *adjective* quick to learn and understand things
cockerel *noun* a male chicken
cockpit *noun* the place in an aircraft where the pilot sits
cockroach *noun* a large dark brown insect with wings
comic strip *noun* a series of drawings that tell a story mostly in pictures
compartment *noun* a section or part of a larger enclosed space
compass *noun* an instrument that shows which direction you are facing
computer generated *adjective* created by computer software
confusion *noun* being puzzled or muddled
consumer *noun* an animal that consumes other animals or plants to survive
control column *noun* the stick that a pilot moves to control the movement of an aircraft
counter *noun* the long table in a shop where customers are served
country *noun* a part of the world where a particular nation of people lives
croquet *noun* a game played on grass where you hit a wooden ball through hoops
cruise *verb* travel gently at a steady speed
cryptosporidiosis *noun* a common waterborne disease caused by a parasite
culture *noun* all the traditions and customs of a group of people
current affairs *plural noun* news about things happening now
curve *noun* a line or surface that bends round, such as the earth's surface
customs *noun* the usual way of doing things

Dd

defence *noun* protecting yourself from criticism or an attack
democracy *noun* a system of government in which all the people can vote to elect their representatives
determined *adjective* having your mind firmly made up
dodge *verb* avoid someone or something by moving quickly
doublecross *verb* deceive someone who trusts you
drama *noun* writing or performing plays
dreamer *noun* a person who wants something badly that they think may happen

Ee

early-learner *noun* a child beginning to learn to read

easy-going *adjective* happy to accept things without worrying or getting angry

edit *verb* choose parts of a film or soundtrack and put them in the right order

editor *noun* someone who prepares a book, newspaper, or magazine for publishing

election *noun* the process of voting for people, especially for members of parliament

emigrate *verb* leave your own country and go and live in another country

envelope *noun* a covering or wrapper

equality *noun* being equal

exist *verb* be present, be alive

experiment *noun* a test that is done to study what happens

exploration *noun* travelling into space or around a country to learn about it

external *adjective* on the outside

extinct *adjective* not alive now

extraordinarily *adverb* unusually

extreme *adjective* very great or very strong

Ff

fabric *noun* a thin material or cloth

fairness *noun* treating all people equally and according to the rules and the law

falconer *noun* a person who trains falcons (birds of prey) to hunt and kill other birds or animals for sport

famous *adjective* known to a lot of people

feel blue *idiom* be sad

fire *verb* put unglazed pottery or clay into a very hot oven and bake it until it is hard

five-penny *adjective, noun* a UK coin

flame *noun* a bright strip of fire

flick *verb* move or hit something with a quick, light movement

flight *noun* the action of flying by an aircraft, rocket or bird

flinch *verb* make a sudden movement because you are frightened or in pain

flock *noun* a group of birds or animals

flutter *noun* a light and flapping movement

fond of *adjective* if you are fond of something or someone, you like them very much

food chain *noun* a series of plants and animals, each of which is eaten as food by the one above in the series
foot *noun* a measurement equal to 30.5cm
for his own sake *idiom* for himself
foreign *adjective* belonging to or coming from another country
fossil *noun* hardened remains of a plant or animal
freedom *noun* the right to go where you like and do what you like
frothy *adjective* if a liquid is frothy, it has a mass of tiny bubbles on or in it
frustration *noun* the feeling of annoyance when you cannot do what you want to do
funny *adjective* something that is funny makes you laugh or smile
furious *adjective* very angry
future *noun* the time that will come

Gg

galactic *adjective* related to a galaxy (a very large group of stars)
gazette *noun* a newspaper
gentle *adjective* kind and quiet, not rough or severe
geography *noun* the science or study of the world and its climate, peoples, and products
glide *verb* fly smoothly, especially without the use of an engine
globe *noun* the world
government *noun* the group of people who are in charge of a country and run it
GPS *noun* global positioning system which uses satellites to find the position of a vehicle or a person ('sat nav')
grasp *verb* hold something or someone tightly
gravity *noun* the force that pulls everything towards the earth
guardian *noun* a person who looks after an orphan

Hh

habitats *noun* the places where animals or plants naturally live or grow
hangar *noun* a large covered space where aircraft are kept
haunting *adjective* staying in your mind
herbivore *noun* an animal that eats only plants
hero *noun* the most important man or boy in a story, film, or play
high-tech *adjective* using the most advanced technology
home plate *noun* (in baseball) the place where the person hitting the ball stands and where they must return to after running around all the bases

honesty *noun* being truthful, without stealing, cheating or telling lies
hose *noun* a long flexible tube through which gas or liquid can travel
hostile *adjective* very unfriendly and ready to fight
huddle *verb* crowd together with other people for warmth or comfort
human rights *plural noun* rights which people think that every living person should have, such as freedom
humanoid robot *noun* a machine which looks like a human
hurtle *verb* move quickly or dangerously

Ii

idea *noun* something that you have thought of
identity *noun* who somebody is
illustrator *noun* a person who produces the illustrations in a book
imagine *verb* form ideas in your mind about things that might happen in the future or might be true
in a jiffy *idiom* very quickly
international *adjective* to do with more than one country
interview *verb* meet with somebody to ask them questions or discuss something
invention *noun* the making of something new that has not existed before
ivory *noun* the hard creamy-white substance that forms elephants' tusks

Jj

jam *verb* when something jams, it becomes stuck and difficult to move
justice *noun* right and fair treatment, for example, as based on the law

Ll

laden *adjective* carrying a heavy load
lament *verb* to express grief or disappointment about something
laptop *noun* a computer small enough to be held and used on your lap
lasso *noun* a rope with a loop at the end, used by cowboys for catching cattle
launch *verb* to make something available for the first time
lawyer *noun* a person whose job is to help people with the law
leech *noun* a small worm that sticks to the skin and sucks out blood
letter *verb* to print or paint letters onto something
liner *noun* a large passenger ship
lively *adjective* cheerful, full of life and energy
Loch Ness monster *noun* an ancient creature which is supposed to live at the bottom of a lake in Scotland

Mm

magazine *noun* a paper publication which comes out regularly, with articles or stories

manga *noun* a comic in the Japanese style

manufacture *verb* make things with machines, usually in a factory

marathon *noun* a long-distance running race on roads

marketing assistant *noun* a person who helps to tell people about a product or service

marvellously *adverb* wonderfully

Maya *noun* an ancient Indian civilization from Central America from about 1000 CE

maze *noun* a confusing network of paths or rivers

microphone *noun* a piece of electrical equipment that picks up sound waves for recording them

mission *noun* a particular journey, such as a journey into space

Mom *noun* American for 'mother'

moment *noun* a very short period of time

mothership *noun* the plane from which other spaceships are launched

motion capture *noun* computer software that records the movements of people and things

motion sensor *noun* an instrument that detects movement

mythology *noun* the study of myths, old stories about gods and heroes in ancient times

Nn

nationality *noun* belonging to a particular country

navigate *verb* make sure that an aircraft, ship or vehicle is going in the right direction

newspaper *noun* a daily or weekly publication of large sheets of printed paper folded together, containing news reports and articles

no small order *idiom* not a small amount

nonviolence *noun* a peaceful way of bringing about change

nuclear reactor *noun* an installation that produces electricity through nuclear energy

nylon *noun* a very strong artificial (man-made) material

Oo

one's *adjective* belonging to a person

oppression *noun* treating people all the time in a cruel, unkind way

optimistic *adjective* expecting things to turn out well

ornithopter *noun* a flying machine

outsmart *verb* do cleverer things than other people

Pp

page-turner *noun* a book that is so exciting or interesting that you have to keep reading it
passion *noun* a great enthusiasm for something, for example, a sport
passport *noun* an official document that allows you to travel abroad
peace *noun* peace is a time when there is no war or violence
pence *plural noun* pennies (UK coins)
personality *noun* your personality is your nature and character
pessimistic *adjective* expecting things to turn out badly
pirate *noun* a sailor who attacks and robs other ships
plonk *verb* put something down clumsily or heavily
plough *verb* crash violently into something
poison *verb* to kill or harm someone or something with a substance
pollute *verb* to make a place or thing dirty or impure
port *noun* the left-hand side of a ship or aircraft when you face forward
potter *noun* someone who makes pots, cups, plates or other things made of baked clay
pounding *adjective* making a very loud repeated noise
precious *adjective* very valuable
predator *noun* an animal that kills and eats other animals
predict *verb* say that something will happen in the future
presentation *noun* a formal talk showing or demonstrations something
pretend *verb* behave as if something untrue or imaginary is real
producer *noun* a plant that produces its own food from sunlight
professional *adjective* doing a certain type of work or sport to earn money
propel *verb* move something rapidly forward, for example, a boat or aircraft
publish *verb* to print and sell books

Rr

rant *verb* to speak or complain about something in a loud and/or angry way
record *noun* the best performance in a sport
reflective *adjective* sending back light or heat
regular feature *noun* a topic which appears each week in a magazine
release *verb* set somebody or something free
remote *adjective* far from anywhere else
retort *noun* a quick or angry reply
rickshaw *noun* a small light two-wheeled carriage pulled by a man, used in Asia to carry passengers

ricochet *verb* bounce off something
roar *verb* make a loud deep sound
rocket *noun* a pointed tube that is pushed into the air by hot gases
roll *verb* move along by turning over and over
rustle *verb* make a gentle sound by moving papers or dry leaves

Ss

sarcastically *adverb* mockingly, by saying the opposite of what you mean
sari *noun* a long length of cloth worn as a dress, especially by Indian women and girls
savour *verb* enjoy the taste or smell of something
scan *verb* read to find specific information
scatter *verb* to throw things in all directions
scientific *adjective* to do with science
scold *verb* speak angrily at someone
scorch *verb* travel at a very high speed; turn something red or brown by making it too hot
scramble *verb* move quickly and clumsily
script *noun* the written text of a play or film
separate *verb* move people apart so that they are no longer together
shoot *verb* fire a gun; move very fast
shuttered *adjective* with the shutters closed, with the light shut out
shuttle *noun* a spacecraft that travels repeatedly between the Earth and a space station
shy *adjective* timid and afraid to meet or talk to other people
skim (read) *verb* read something quickly to get a general idea of the subject
smart *adjective* clever
So there! *idiom* an expression of firmness
solo *adverb* by yourself
sonny *noun* friendly name for a boy
sounding *adjective* producing a sound, especially of a loud and pleasant nature
soundproof *adjective* made so that no sound can get in or out
soundtrack *noun* the recorded sound, including speech and music, in a film
spaceman *noun* a man who travels in a spacecraft
spaceport *noun* an airport for spaceships
sponsor *verb* to promise to give someone money if they do something difficult and give money to charity
spread *verb* lay something out to its full size

sprint *verb* run or move very fast for a short distance
squawk *verb* when a bird squawks, it makes a loud harsh cry
squeamish *adjective* easily disgusted, for example, at the sight of blood
squint *verb* look at something with half-shut eyes
starboard *noun* the right-hand side of a ship or aircraft when you face forward
steal home (or 'steal base') *verb* (in baseball) running to a base or to the home plate before another player from your team hits the ball
storyboard *noun* a series of drawings to show the plot of a film, or action in a film
struggle *noun* a great effort, a fight
sure glad *adjective* very pleased
survive *verb* continue to live
suspend *verb* hang something below something else
swarm *verb* bees or other insects swarm when they fly or move about together in groups
swat *verb* hit or crush a fly or other insect
swerve *verb* move suddenly to one side
swift *adjective* quick, fast
swing, swung, swung *verb* move in a curve
system *noun* a way of doing something, for example, in politics

Tt

tabloid format *noun* with square pages
technical *adjective* to do with technology or the way things work
Think nothing of it! *idiom* Don't worry about it.
throne *noun* a special chair for a king, queen or emperor
throng *verb* when a crowd of people throng a place, for example, a square in a city, they fill it
toga *noun* a long loose piece of clothing worn by men in ancient Rome
totter *verb* walk unsteadily or wobble
trail *verb* hang down
trailer *noun* a truck or wheeled container that is pulled by a car or lorry
tribe *noun* a group of people who live together and are ruled by a chief
trickster *noun* a person who plays tricks on others
truth *noun* something that is true (believed to be something that actually exists, or happened)
tsunami *noun* a big wave caused by an earthquake
tumble *verb* fall down clumsily
typhoon *noun* a very strong storm at sea

Vv

velociraptor *noun* a medium-sized, feathered dinosaur. It means 'swift seizer'

violence *noun* the use of force to hurt or kill people

Vishnu *noun* a Hindu god

vow *verb* make a serious promise

Ww

wail *verb* cry out with a long sad cry

weightlessness *noun* being free of the Earth's gravity and without weight, so that you float about

whisk *verb* move something away quickly and suddenly

willow pattern *noun* a traditional blue and white pattern on chinaware telling a story

wingspan *noun* the distance across the wings of an aeroplane

wisdom *noun* being wise (knowing or understanding many things)

witness *verb* watch

wolf (down) *verb* eat something in a very quick and hungry way

Yy

yacht *noun* a sailing boat with a cabin for sleeping

Zz

zip on his wit *idiom* very fast thinker

My vocabulary list

My vocabulary list

My vocabulary list

My vocabulary list

My vocabulary list

My vocabulary list